POLICE WITHOUT BORDERS

MAGAZINE

July/August 2015

In Search of Balance Issue

Law Enforcement Officers

Digital Life:

policewithoutborderders.com

Publication

Table of Content

On sale at amazon.com

Books Category, search for My Connections Magazine. For best quality printing

Policewithoutborders.com is part of the weconnect2.com digital network about social and practical issues evolve around people lives.

This Law Enforcement Officers publications focus on the Police

Community at large. Local, regional,

1

nationwide, and world wide good and bad situations LEO are faced with on a daily basis.

On the cover
Featured True Cop Story:

Big Fat Turkey

"Working a slow up in the mountains. I stopped a car where I thought the occupant may have been in possession of a gun. So I called for another deputy. Soon after, I heard my partner answer up on the radio and began to respond. Well, he just around the corner from me when I heard him on the radio say, " I copy, show me enroute, ahh F*ck!!!!" and then dead silence over the radio. My heart stopped and all I could do is guess and speculate what could have possibly happened to him. A carwreck? god forbid an ambush? what could it have been... The dispatcher quickly got on the radio and asked "4-2, are you code 4?" at that point I knew that every cop in the County was in suspense, waiting... everything was put on hold... My partner replied back he was out of breath and you could hear the lingering fear in his voice. He stuttered "affirm, I am...

code 4, I thought... I hit a animal,.. but I... did'nt..." No cop in the County knew what he was talking about, all we knew was that he was ok. He assisted me on my car stop, but the entire time he was distracted and had appeared as if he had a near death experience or had seen a ghost. After clearing the stop, he told me what he had seen and then drove me to where it happened. Mountain kids get pretty bored and... creative in the winter. Several kids contructed

we connect 2

weconnect2.com
buyers+sellers

several over sized cardboard cut-outs of real looking animals, cats, dogs, coyotes and conviently placed them all over the mountain roads. They propped them up on sticks and tied ropes to them as they hid behind trees or ditches. As my partner drove by they yanked the rope making it appear as if it was moving. I feel it is appropriate to accurately describe the exact demimsions and "size" of certain body parts on the card board animal my partner hit. The genitalia on the cat/coyote was approximately 16"... As I stood over the cut out I could not stop from laughing, and laughing and luaghing at my partner....and the situation. He was bitter and was not amused...He spent that last 3 hours of the shift tracking down the kids....he was succesful. In my book the kids should get a

 "get out of jail" free card due to their great creativity..."

True cop story from around the web.

Ask a cop

In this Tuesday, May 26, 2015 photo, Cleveland Mayor Frank Jackson speaks at a news conference announcing the settlement agreement with the City of Cleveland. (AP Image)

policewithoutborders.com

ASK A COP::::::<<<<<<<<<<<<<<<<<<<
<<<<<<<<Civilians get new authority in Cleveland PD settlement
Calls for civilians to play influential roles in investigating police misconduct and establishing policies and procedures

<<<<<<<<<<<<<<<<<<<<<<<<
By Mark Gillispie
Associated Press

CLEVELAND — Cleveland's settlement agreement with the U.S. Department of Justice on reforming the city's troubled police department calls for civilians to play influential roles in investigating police misconduct and establishing policies and procedures.

The city and Justice Department announced Tuesday that they'd reached a settlement on a consent decree that a federal judge must approve and an independent monitor will enforce. DOJ officials said in December that an 18-month investigation had found that Cleveland police had engaged in a pattern of excessive force and civil rights violations.

In this Tuesday, May 26, 2015 photo, Cleveland Mayor Frank Jackson speaks at a news conference announcing the settlement agreement with the City of Cleveland. (AP Image) RELATED ARTICLES Community policing at center of Cleveland reform plan Cleveland reaches settlement with DOJ over police conduct RELATED CONTENT SPONSORED BY

The 105-page agreement details new rules for how officers employ, report and investigate uses of deadly and nonlethal force, to include prohibitions against shooting at moving vehicles, striking suspects in the head with their firearms and using stun guns to inflict pain, examples of which were cited in the DOJ investigative findings. The

agreement also requires Cleveland police to make

On Sale at amazon.com

community policing, which requires officers to work with citizens and to help them solve problems when possible, its core principle.

A striking component of the decree is the level of civilian authority in vital areas of police administration and oversight.

The agreement calls for a civilian to head the internal affairs unit, rather than a member of the police command staff. And a civilian will be appointed to the new position of police inspector

general. No former employees of

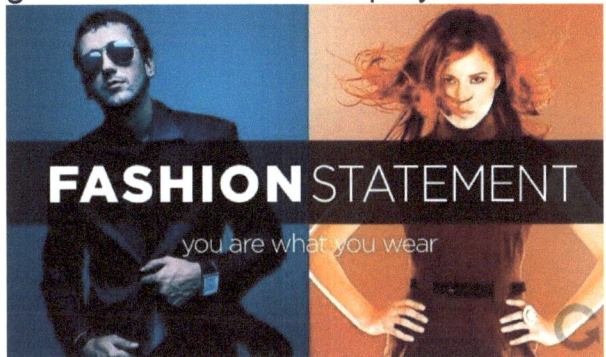

Myconnectionsmagazine.com

About fashion communications at all levels. Body language, diet, travel, trends. Visit and endulge your mind……

the Cleveland police department can hold those positions.

Additionally, a community police commission consisting of 10 civilians and a representative from each of the three police unions will be formed. According to the settlement, the commission will have the authority to review, recommend and comment on police department policies, procedures and performance, along with its adherence required reforms.

"It's fair to say the city has committed in this consent decree a vigorous civilian and community component in the way we're going to police in Cleveland," U.S. Attorney Steven Dettelbach said in an interview with The Associated Press. "An important

point to me going forward is that the community and department will be linked in many ways that hasn't occurred before."

A city spokesman said the administration would not comment at this time.

Many large cities and police departments across the nation have internal affairs units, inspector general's offices and civilian review boards that serve as watchdog agencies.

Appointing a civilian to lead the internal affairs unit in Cleveland appears to be tied to DOJ findings that criticized the city for its inability or unwillingness to punish officers for wrongdoing. The report singled out internal affairs, concluding in its findings that the unit "failed to ask key questions and take important investigatory steps."

"In some cases, these flaws prevented the (department) from holding officers accountable for serious misconduct," the report said.

Dettelbach said the head of internal affairs will answer to the police chief and will provide "a fresh perspective" on criminal investigations of police.

The police inspector general will have wide-ranging authority to investigate whatever he or she wishes. Dettelbach described the position as an "internal whistleblower" whose investigative findings are not binding. The consent decree calls for the inspector general to work out of the mayor's office and answer to the police chief.

The community police commission, Dettelbach said, could become an incubator for ideas on how to make the department better.

"The hope is that it will be a body that is saying things that are important and relevant and are backed by data," he said.

A law professor said Tuesday that Cleveland's ceding of police authority to civilians shows that the department and city administrations have long done a poor job of policing the police. Michael Benza of the Case Western Reserve University School of Law said in an interview that the new civilian roles should be about more than community policing, a policy that requires officers to be engaged with the people they serve.

"There's also a need to have the community connected and to feel empowered to make substantive changes in how they want the police department to work," Benza said.

Copyright 2015 The Associated Press>>

Public Safety Tips for travelers or tourists:

1- Don't Trust People Too Quickly

When you're traveling in a new destination, and especially when you're traveling on your own, it can be tempting to join up and find a tribe. Sometimes these tribes turn into lifelong friendships.

2-Spend Extra Money on Staying Safe

If you're traveling long-term on a shoestring budget, it can be hard to justify spending extra cash when it could go toward so many more fun activities. But it's a smart idea to financially invest in your own safety

3- **When you are out in public**

The same rules you would use at home to avoid becoming a crime victim apply here. Avoiding certain areas, keeping track of your cash and credit cards, and dealing with businesses you know and trust are some basic tourist safety tips. We like to say... "Common sense, don't leave home without it!

A to Z safety tips:

While out in public

- Do not display large amounts of money. Place small amounts in different pockets to assist with this or use credit cards or travelers checks.

- Make copies of your credit cards front and back and place them in a secured place for your records (room safe). This can be very useful if you need to report a lost or stolen card.

- If you see something suspicious, call 911 immediately. When you return to your hotel, use the main entrance especially in the evening.

- Be wary of solicitors. Use reputable places of business for all your entertainment transactions.

- Travel in pairs or groups if possible.

- Always have a meeting place for the kids to meet you if they get lost.

- Teach your kids your name, house phone and cell phone number.

- Small children should always be led by the hand when crossing the road or near busy streets.

- Small children should have their name and phone number placed on their clothes label or the inside of a shoe flap with a permanent marker in case they are lost.

- Use the sidewalk and pedestrian crossings.

Source: Orange County Sheriff's office.

CONTACT YOUR LOCAL POLICE DEPARTMENT FOR ANY PUBLIC SAFETY CONCERNS. EVERY CITY, TOWN, COMMUNITY HAVE DIFFERENT PUBLIC SAFETY CONCERNS.

So, what happened in Los Angeles Stay in New york

This apply on about everything and everywhere. When we mix milk with soda we get milk and soda mixed together. Try it sometimes and that's what you end up with.

Problems and situations in las Vegas are more of Las vegas problems than Dallas's problems. Yes, one can read about, watch, and even share problems with others, but the bottom line is that not to make them your own. For example, if a situation involved a cop in New York with a pedestrian from Germany, we all hope that this will not travel to Berlin and become a German Police problem with an American Pedestrian. Let's stop here. So our problems doesn't travel any further as simple as it sound. By Eddie Elchahed, Editor PWB MAG

Police Brutality

What is and what is not?

From an expert point of view:

Police brutality is the wanton use of excessive force, usually physical, but also common in forms of verbal attacks and psychological intimidation, by a police officer.

Widespread police brutality exists in many countries, even those that prosecute it.[1] It is one of several forms of police misconduct, which include: false arrest; intimidation; racial profiling; political repression; surveillance abuse; sexual abuse; and police corruption.[2] Although illegal, it can be done under the color of law.

Source is the Wikipedia The Free Encyclopedia

Causes

Ian Tomlinson after being pushed to the ground by police in London (2009). He collapsed and died soon after.

Protest against police brutality after the eviction of unemployed demonstrators occupying the Post Office in Vancouver, Canada, 1938

Police officers are legally permitted to use force, and their superiors—and the public — expect them to do so. According to Jerome Herbert Skolnick, in dealing largely with disorderly elements of the society, some people working in law enforcement may gradually develop an attitude or sense of authority over society, particularly under traditional reaction-based policing models; in some cases

the police believe that they are above the law.[33]

There are many reasons as to why police officers are excessively aggressive to civilians. It is thought that some personality traits make some officers more susceptible to the use of excessive force than others. In one study police psychologists were surveyed on officers who had used excessive force. The information obtained allowed the researchers to develop five unique types of officers, only one of which was similar to the bad apple stereotype.

FBI Director James Comey : He was the United States Deputy Attorney General, serving in PresidentGeorge W. Bush's administration. As Deputy Attorney General, Comey was the second-highest-ranking official in the United States Department of Justice(DOJ) and ran the day-to-day operations of the Department, serving in that office from December 2003 through August

2005. He was U.S. Attorney for the Southern District of New York prior to becoming Deputy Attorney General.

In December 2003, as Deputy Attorney General, Comey appointed the U.S. Attorney in Chicago, close friend and former colleague Patrick Fitzgerald, as Special Counsel to head the CIA leak grand jury investigation after Attorney General John Ashcroft recused himself. In August 2005, Comey left the DOJ and he became General Counsel and Senior Vice President of Lockheed Martin. In 2010, he became General Counsel at Bridgewater Associates. In early 2013, he left Bridgewater to become Senior Research Scholar andHertog Fellow on National Security Law at Columbia Law School. He also joined the London-based board of directors of HSBC Holdings.

United States Law Enforcement officers 2014 fatalities increased.

The FBI publishes an annual report using information on officer deaths reported by its field offices, law enforcement agencies and nonprofits. From 2004 to 2013, an average of 114 officers died each year. The FBI breaks down the figure in two ways: accidents and "felonious incidents," or deaths as a result of a criminal act. Accidental deaths include aircraft accidents, being struck by vehicles while directing traffic, drownings and being shot accidentally in a crossfire. Felonious incidents include ambushes, traffic pursuits and responding to domestic violence or barricades, hostage-taking or arrest situations.

A CBS interview revealed that the "anger and the hatred and the violence" directed against police officers take more than 100 officers' lives. On average, 114 officers died in the line of duty every year from 2004 to 2013, according to FBI data. The lowest was 76 deaths in 2013, and the highest was 140 in 2007.

In general, law enforcement fatalities have been declining

since the 1970s. Some factors that contributed to the decline were increased use of bullet-resistant vests, availability of highly-trained SWAT teams that are used for especially dangerous situations, and use of stun guns that allow officers to keep a distance from perpetrators instead of hand-to-hand combat.

Felonious deaths also have been on a steady decline. Nearly 140 officers died in felonious incidents in 1973. In 2013, there were 27 such deaths, according to the FBI. Ambush attacks, which certainly fit Bratton's description, accounted for 21.7 percent of felonious deaths from 2004 to 2013:

(FBI Law Enforcement Officers Killed and Assaulted, 2013 report)

NYPD cited the figure using the National Law Enforcement Officers Memorial Fund's 2014 annual report, according to a spokesman who declined to be identified. The nonprofit tracks officer deaths and publishes an annual report that breaks down the causes of death. The 2014 preliminary report, released in December, contains the memorial fund's unofficial findings from the year. The FBI has not yet published its 2014 Law Enforcement Officers Killed and Assaulted report.

The total number of deaths reported by the memorial fund is consistently higher than FBI data. One factor contributing to the higher number is the memorial fund's count of job-related illnesses, such as heart attacks. But such data also would not support Bratton's claim of "anger and the hatred and the violence directed against our police officers."

In 2014, 126 officers died while on duty, according to the memorial fund. Half of the officers were killed in felonious incidents. Of the 62 felonious incidents, 15 were ambushes similar to the killings of the two NYPD officers. The other half resulted from non-criminal incidents such as accidents and job-related illnesses.

Ambushes triggered by anti-government or anti-police sentiment started "well before" the protests over the deaths of Michael Brown in Ferguson and Eric Garner in Staten Island, said Craig Floyd, chairman and chief executive of the memorial fund. For example, two Las Vegas police officers were fatally shot point-blank while eating lunch at a Cici's Pizza by a couple who had expressed anti-government views. A sniper attack by an anti-police survivalist killed one Pennsylvania state trooper and injured another when they were standing outside the police barracks.

In 2010, the Justice Department launched a training program calledVALOR (Violence Against Law Enforcement and Ensuring Officer Resilience and Survivability) to address increases in ambush-style assaults of police.

Lastly, it is important to note the context to these numbers. There were about 627,000 law enforcement officers in 2013, according to the FBI. If 62 officers were killed as a result of criminal acts in 2014, that would make up 0.01 percent of U.S. police forces.

The percentage of homicides of police is lower compared to some other occupations in the United States, including retail sales workers and food preparation workers, according to the Bureau of Labor Statistics. (Clarification: The BLS table shows homicides as a percentage of total fatal injuries for the specific occupation group, not compared to the total labor force in that group.) The rate of nonfatal occupational injury and illness among police, at least in local government, was **among** the highest in 2013.

England

Police deaths: The officers killed in the line of duty

The deaths of Fiona Bone, 32, and Nicola Hughes, 23, during a routine operation in Tameside, Greater Manchester, are the latest in a long list of UK police fatalities.

It is the first such incident to involve two female officers.

Speaking about their deaths, Greater Manchester Chief Constable Sir Peter Fahy said: "Day in, day out, police officers go about their duty, go into dangerous situations, unexpected situations, and show great bravery, great courage and are with people at the very worst moments in their lives.

"This is exactly what these two officers were doing."

According to the National Memorial Day organisation, more than 4,000 police officers have been killed in the line of duty

since 1792, when the first salaried constables went on duty.

The organisation said 256, including PC Bone and PC Hughes, have been shot since 1945.

Joe Holness, who founded the organisation, said the figures rose each year by an average of between 10 and 15 officers.

The charity, **Police Roll of Honour Trust**, has named every UK officer who has been killed in the line of duty.

They include PC Sharon Beshenivsky who was shot dead during a bungled robbery in Morley Street, Bradford, on 18 November 2005.

Two men were jailed for life for her murder. She had been responding to an armed robbery

call with fellow PC
Teresa Milburn.

PC Beshenivsky had been a police officer for just nine months and became the first female officer in 20 years to be shot dead by a criminal in England and Wales.

In one of the most notorious incidents of all - almost five decades ago, in 1966 - armed robber Harry Roberts and an accomplice shot and killed three officers.

Det Con David Wombwell, Sgt Christopher Head and PC Geoffrey Fox died when they stopped a van in Shepherd's Bush, west London.

Other more recent high-profile deaths include PC Alison Armitage, 29, who died after being run over twice by the driver of a stolen car in the car park of a derelict pub in Oldham, in 2001.

Thomas Whaley, 19, denied her murder and was jailed for eight years after pleading guilty to manslaughter.

US marine

PC Ian Broadhurst was shot dead after stopping a motorist on Boxing Day in Leeds in 2003.

David Bieber, a former US marine, was jailed for life for murder after Newcastle Crown Court heard the 34-year-old officer was shot in the head at point blank range despite pleading for his life.

Police officers killed in the line of duty

- More than 4,000 since 1792

- UK including Northern Ireland since 1945: 256 shot and 21 stabbed

- England: 51 shot and 19 stabbed

- Wales: none

- Scotland: four shot and two stabbed

- Northern Ireland: 201 shot

Source: National Police Memorial Day website

In 2003, PC Stephen Oake was repeatedly stabbed during an anti-terror raid in Manchester. He was holding on to Algerian national Kamel Bourgass during the operation, to stop him escaping.

Bourgass was sentenced to life in prison on 29 June 2004 for the murder of PC Oake and the attempted murder of three other Greater Manchester officers.

Northumbria Police officer PC Joe Carroll, 46, died following a crash on the A69 near Hexham in April 2006 as a prisoner tried to escape from his patrol car.

Army instructor Steven Graham, 39, was jailed for five-and-a-half years for his manslaughter.

In 2007, 37-year-old PC Gary Toms from the Metropolitan Police died after suffering serious head injuries while investigating a robbery.

Armed officers had attempted to stop a car in Stratford, east London and followed it to Ashlin Road in Newham.

In 2008, PC Ian Terry, 32, from Burnley died after being shot in the chest by a Greater Manchester Police colleague during a training exercise at a disused factory.

PC Terry's widow, Joanne, has said she is "bitterly disappointed" no-one will face criminal charges over his death.

Killed in training

Drug addict David Parfitt was found guilty of manslaughter after PC Ged Walker died after being dragged more than 100 yards trailing from a car door before suffering fatal injuries.

Parfitt, who was at the wheel of a stolen taxi when he dragged the officer at a speed of 30mph along a street in Bulwell, Nottingham, was jailed for 13 years.

Father-of-three Stephen Oake, a 40-year-old plain-clothed special branch officer, was stabbed in the chest and died soon afterwards in hospital in 2003.

Four others were injured during a counter terrorism operation in Manchester.

Officers had been arresting a man in a raid linked to the discovery of the deadly poison ricin in London when they were attacked after holding him for an hour.

Traffic officer PC Jon Odell, who lived in Margate, died in hospital after being dragged about 50 yards down a road while carrying out speed checks in December 2000.

His hat, shoes, belt, baton and CS spray were strewn along the path of the car, and driver Wayne Rule, 25, was jailed for nine years after admitting manslaughter.

In 2004, Det Con Michael Swindells, 44, died from a single stab wound in Birmingham.

Police admitted he had not been wearing a stab-proof vest when he was attacked on a canal tow path which heads under the M6 toward Spaghetti Junction.

Earlier this year PC Ian Dibell, 41, of Essex Police was killed while taking action, despite being off duty.

He had intervened in an incident close to his home in Clacton-on-Sea to protect a member of the public from an armed man. PC Dibell was shot dead.

PC David Rathband, who was found dead earlier this year, had been shot in the face and blinded by fugitive Raoul Moat in July 2010 while sitting in his patrol car in Newcastle.

The Usual Suspects? Study Finds Majority of Police Abuse Cases Involve Same Small Group Of Officers

Chicago Police:

There is an interesting study out that a relatively small number of officers are responsible for over half of police abuse claims. We have seen similar results in studies of malpractice cases of doctors. Yet, this small group of officers not only tarnish the reputations of all officers but cost massive amounts of money. **Marketplace reports** that Chicago paid out more than half a billion dollars over 10 years in police misconduct cases. This is a city that is facing junk bond status and the threat of insolvency.

Law professor Craig Futterman, who runs the University of Chicago's Civil Rights and Police Accountability Project, has done some interesting work in this area. His study of the Chicago Police Department found the same officers fueling these costs. It suggests that a better job of self-policing could result in substantial savings for police departments and more importantly greater protection for citizens.

UCLA law professor Joanna Schwartz has found similar results. She notes however that most cities still resist keeping records that would help identify such officers and track patterns.

This would seem to offer obvious areas of reform for departments. We have certainly seen anecdotally that officers involved in controversies often seem to have checkered histories of prior lawsuits or serious complaints. The problem is the political will to implement the academic findings.

Below some comments on the Study:

1. **Pogo Hears a Who**

   "Chicago paid out more than half a billion dollars over 10 years in police misconduct cases"

   This won't be addressed until the Police force itself pays these claims out of their budget.

   As it stands now, "Chicago" (i.e., taxpayers) pay for this, so why should the Police care?

   No consequences, no change.

2. **Ross**

Weren't "Sovereign Immunity" protections only designed for constitutional and legal activities made in good faith? Why should taxpayers pay for any of it?

3. **Olly**

Where's the study on Lawyers?

-Study Public Safety World Wide And cause of death

The World Health Organization's *Global Status Report on Road Safety 2013* tabulates 1.24 million deaths worldwide:

Traffic accidents kill 1.24 million people a year worldwide; wars and murders, 0.44 million.

THE NUMBERS: Annual deaths* from –

Cause	World
Traffic Accidents	1,240,000
Homicide	437,000
Military conflict	55,000

* 2010 estimates for world, 2012 for the United States

WHAT THEY MEAN:

Google tests a driverless car with no steering wheel; Honda introduces an auto-pilot-backed Accord to Australia; —Cruisell offers a $10,000 upgrade-to-autopilot feature for Bay Area Audis; Ford has its own plans. Auto-industry writer Dale Buss scoffs, writing in *Forbes* magazine that with auto fatalities trending down, at least on safety grounds there's no need for anything radically new:

—It's bogus to assert that driverless cars are required to address the issue of traffic accidents and fatalities. The number of U.S. auto-crash fatalities was declining steadily for years until very recently, when distracted driving, thanks largely to texting, reared its ugly head. But surely there are less drastic solutions to that development than removing every American driver from behind the wheel.‖

True enough, auto fatalities have been heading down in the United States. Better manufacturing, safety regulations, and changing social attitudes on alcohol and seat-belts have cut the National Highway Traffic Safety

Administration's traffic death count rapidly and deeply, from the mid-1970s peak of 55,000 to 45,000 deaths in 2006, 32,885 in 2011 – the lowest number of traffic deaths since 1949 – and 33,561 in 2012.

So, significantly lower numbers.

But —lowerǁ shouldn't be confused with —low.ǁ An annual U.S. rate of 33,000 deaths (which includes 2,700 teenagers) is six times the annual number of deaths to HIV/AIDS, double the annual deaths to murder, and comparable to the casualty rates for the Korean War or World War I. Put another way, using state traffic figures, nine Texans die daily in car crashes, three each week Maine, one daily in Kansas, two per day in Illinois, and so on.

And worldwide, the U.S. is actually relatively safe. The World Health Organization's Global Status Report on Road Safety 2013 estimates 1.24 million traffic deaths a year – nearly triple the UN's estimate of annual murders,

and twenty times the estimated annual total of deaths in wars. The toll is highest in middle-income countries, as a riskily picturesque mix of vehicles – cars, scooters, small motorcycles, trishaws, sometimes farm animals and carts – combines with the absence of helmet laws, and weaker police and emergency medical services. The worldwide traffic fatality rate is about 17 per 100,000 people – 50 percent above the 11.4 percent in the U.S., and likely higher if a world figure for deaths per vehicle-mile were available.

Why do all these crashes happen? NHTSA believes —human error is the critical reason for 93 percent of crashes.ǁ A Missouri review of the state's 716 fatal crashes in 2011 found equipment or road failures responsible for 11, while the other 705 involved human error – typically some combination of speeding, drinking, bad lane changes, and so on.

Now, back to the driverless car. Options range from Google's experiment with the fully ‗autonomous‘ vehicle to more evolutionary changes, in which an _autopilot' guides most driving decisions, and the _Internet of things' enables cars to sense approaching objects, scooters, people and stop by themselves. In principle, removing the driver can eliminate accidents resulting from drunkenness, drug use, texting, falling asleep, jumping red lights, looking left while a headphone-wearing pedestrian walks into your way from the right, and other human errors

No doubt, the concept raises engineering challenges, software questions, and marketing questions. Certainly after 120 years of eyes on the road and hands on the wheel, it is _radical.' But assuming the rate of human error in fatal crashes is essentially the same as that in crashes overall, in principle driverless cars could cut deaths by 90 percent in the U.S.. Reductions worldwide would likely be smaller in percentage terms, since so many developing-world traffic deaths are in scooter, motorbike, or trishaw accidents. But even a reduction by half would save many more lives than the abolition of murder and war. In which case,

a radical idea – even a —drastic‖ idea – might be a very good one.

- WHO finds American roads a bit more dangerous than those in other rich countries, with a rate of 11.4 traffic deaths per 100,000 people – a level comparable to upper-middle income countries like Poland and Chile. (This could overstate U.S. risk, as the Report covers only deaths per capita, rather than per vehicle-mile.) The world's lowest traffic-fatality rate are in a few small island countries

– the Maldives and Micronesia in particular – where few people own cars. Setting them aside as special cases, the lowest rate is Iceland's 2.8 per 100,000; others include the U.K.'s 3.7 per 100,000, Germany's 4.7, and Japan's 5.2.

The highest rate in the world is the Dominican Republic's 42 deaths per 100,000 people. This attributable in particular to very high and unsafe use of motorcycles: 57% of DR traffic deaths are drivers of, or passengers on, motorcycles or scooters; 25% are pedestrians, and 14% are automobile drivers. Other high rates include 38 deaths per 100,000 in Thailand (74 percent are tuk-tuk or motorcycle drivers or passengers); 37 per 100,000 in Venezuela and Iran, and 34 per 100,000 in Nigeria.

The National Highway Traffic Safety Administration on American traffic fatalities, up to 2012.

Global Study on Homicide

United Nation Office on Crime and Drugs

The global average homicide rate stands at 6.2 per 100,000 population, but Southern Africa and Central America have rates over four times higher than that (above 24 victims per 100,000 population), making them the sub-regions with the highest homicide rates on record, followed by South America, Middle Africa and the Caribbean (between 16 and 23 homicides per 100,000 population). Meanwhile, with rates some five times lower than the global average, Eastern Asia, Southern Europe and Western Europe are the subregions with the lowest homicide levels. Almost three

billion people live in an expanding group of countries with relatively low homicide rates, many of which, particularly in Europe and Oceania, have continued to experience a decrease in their homicide rates since 1990. At the opposite end of the scale, almost 750 million people live in countries with high homicide levels, meaning that almost half of all homicides occur in countries that make up just 11 per cent of the global population and that personal security is still a major concern for more than 1 in 10 people on the planet. A widening gap in homicide levels exists between countries with high homicide rates and those with low homicide rates. There are also notable disparities in homicide within regions and sub-regions, as individual countries follow different paths over time. For example, homicide rates in the southern part of South America are closer to the relatively low rates recorded in Europe, while the rates in the north of the sub-region are closer to the relatively high rates recorded in Central America. Likewise, at the sub-national level, the most populous city in the vast majority of countries generally records higher homicide rates than elsewhere, with notable exceptions being certain countries in Eastern Europe. Certain regions and sub-regions have experienced sustained high levels of homicide. This is particularly notable in the Americas, where homicide levels have been high, and in some cases increasing, over the past decade. But this is not a new Homicide victims and population, by countries' level of homicide per

100,000 population (2012 or latest year) Source: UNODC Homicide Statistics (2013). Al N

pattern, as the Americas have had homicide rates five to eight times higher than those in Europe and Asia since the mid-1950s. The continuing high levels of homicide in the Americas are the legacy of decades of political and crime-related violence, which has hindered a decline in homicide levels in certain countries. However, homicide levels in some countries in the Americas, such as Brazil, are now stabilizing, albeit at a high level, while in other regions, countries with historically high homicide rates, such as South Africa, Lesotho, the Russian

Federation and countries in Central Asia, are managing to break their own cycle of violence and have recorded decreases in their homicide rates. At the opposite end of the spectrum, in countries with some of the lowest homicide rates in the world, mostly located in Europe and Eastern Asia, homicide levels continue to decline. Many of those countries had low levels of homicide in 1995 and have subsequently recorded continuous decreases in their homicide rates. On the other hand, a worrying development is that homicide levels in Northern Africa are rising, probably as a result of political violence, which may in turn foster lethal violence related to criminal activities, and should be monitored. The same can be said for parts of Southern Asia and Eastern Africa. The gender bias Polarization not only exists in terms of where homicide occurs, but also in the sex of its victims and perpetrators. In the context of family and intimate partner relationships, women are considerably more at risk than men, yet 79 per cent of all homicide victims globally are male. Moreover, some 95 per cent of homicide perpetrators at the global level are also male; a share that is consistent across countries and regions, irrespective of the homicide typology or weapon used. The global male homicide rate is almost four times that of females (9.7 versus 2.7 per 100,000) and is highest in the Americas (29.3 per 100,000 males), where it is nearly seven times higher than in Asia, Europe and Oceania (all under 4.5 per 100,000 males). This is due in large part to the higher levels of homicide related to organized crime and gangs in the Americas than in other regions. When factoring in the finding that 43 per cent of all homicide victims are aged 15-29, this means that more than one in seven of all homicide victims globally is a young male aged 15-29 living in the Americas.

There is a regional and gender bias towards male victims in homicide related to organized crime and gangs, but interpersonal homicide in the form of intimate partner/family-related homicide is far more evenly distributed across regions and is, on average, remarkably stable at the global level.

However, intimate partner/family-related homicide disproportionately affects women: two thirds of its victims globally are female (43,600 in 2012) and one third (20,000) are male. Almost half (47 per cent) of all female victims of homicide in 2012 were killed by their intimate partners or family members, compared to less than 6 per cent of male homicide victims. Thus while a large share of female homicide victims are murdered by people who are expected to care for them, the majority of men are killed by people they may not even know. Youth at risk Something that the majority of male and female homicide victims do have in common is their relative youth. The 15-29 and 30-44 age groups account for the vast majority of homicides globally, with almost half of all homicide victims aged 15-29 and slightly less than a third aged 30-44. The homicide rate for male victims aged 15-29 in South America and Central America is more than four times the global average rate for that age group. The 30-44 age group is, however, at higher risk in some countries in Central America, the Caribbean and all sub-regions in

Europe. The impact of this dynamic can be devastating for security and the economy, as the deaths of males in the 30-44 age group can have a disproportionate impact on families, the working population and perceptions of security. At the youngest end of the age spectrum, 36,000 children under the age of 15 were the victims of homicide worldwide in 2012. Equating to 8 per cent of all homicide victims, this coupled with the share of victims in the 15-29 age group (43 per cent) means that more than half of all global homicide victims are under 30 years of age. The many faces of homicide Based on elements including premeditation, motivation, context, instrumentality and the relationship between victim and perpetrator, this study identifies three distinct homicide typologies in order to shed light on different types of lethal violence: homicide related to other criminal activities; homicide related to interpersonal conflict; and homicide related to socio-political agendas. Homicide related to other criminal activities registers very different levels across the world's regions, but there are currently very

high levels of killings of that nature in areas of Central and South America, which are often linked to violence between Percentage distribution of victims of homicide, by sex and selected age group (2012 or latest year) Source: UNODC Homicide Statistics (2013). Americas 15% Total homicide victims (100%) Male homicide victims not 15-29 (44%) Male homicide victims aged 15-29 (35%) Female homicide victims not 15-29 (13%) Female homicide victims aged 15-29 (8%) 15 EXECUTIVE SUMMARY organized criminal groups. Overall, organized crime/gang-related homicide accounts for 30 per cent of homicides in the Americas, compared to less than 1 per cent in Asia, Europe and Oceania, but that does not necessarily mean that organized crime or gangs are more prevalent in the Americas than in other regions. Moreover, levels of organized crime/gang-related homicide can fluctuate dramatically, even in the short term, to the extent that they actually drive changes in homicide rates in some countries in Central America and the Caribbean. On the other hand, homicide committed during the course of other criminal acts appears to be more stable across the world, with homicide linked to robbery accounting for an average of 5 per cent of all homicides in the Americas, Europe and Oceania each year. Not all homicide in the Americas is linked to other criminal activities, however: homicide related to interpersonal conflict also accounts for a significant share of homicides. In Montevideo, Uruguay, for example, the share of interpersonal homicides is higher than the share of crime-related homicides; and in Quito, Ecuador, the shares of those two different typologies are almost identical.1 Interpersonal homicide accounts for a significant share of homicides around the world (for example, Costa Rica: 47 per cent; India: 48 per cent; Sweden: 54 per cent), and it has completely different drivers to homicide related to other criminal activities, often being a means of resolving a conflict and/or punishing the victim through violence when relationships come under strain. Intimate partner/family-related homicide is one form of interpersonal homicide that affects

every country, irrespective of affluence, development and both risk and protective factors, which can mitigate levels of lethal violence. Accounting for 14 per cent of all homicides globally, intimate partner/family-related homicide has the greatest intensity in the Americas, whereas it accounts for a larger share of all homicides in Asia, Europe and Oceania, where those most at risk are women aged 30 and over. Other types of interpersonal homicide, such as property disputes or revenge-type killings, also occur all around the globe. More difficult to quantify than the other two typologies, homicide related to socio-political agendas is committed in order to exert influence over power relationships and to advance a particular agenda. This type of homicide can draw a lot of 1 Banco Interamericano de Desarollo (2013). attention due to its often shocking nature — as in the case of acts of terror leading to death — and can represent a substantive share of total homicides in specific contexts or regions, such as in postconflict settings or during periods of instability. War and conflict-related killings are also considered socio-political violence, but are not included in this category as they are outside the realm of intentional homicide. External cross-cutting factors A number of factors intervene in the process that leads to the commission of homicide. Ranging from the availability of a weapon (or lack of one) to the use of psychoactive substances, which may act as homicide "enablers", such elements can shape patterns and levels of homicide, and when they are targeted by prevention policies, homicide can be reduced. Not all homicides involve them, but weapons do play a significant role in homicide. With their high level of lethality,2 firearms are the most widely used weapons, accounting for 4 out of every 10 homicides at the global level, whereas "other means", such as physical force and blunt objects, among others, kill just over a third of homicide victims, while sharp objects kill a quarter. The use of firearms is particularly prevalent in the Americas, where two thirds of homicides are committed with guns, whereas sharp objects are used more frequently in Oceania and Europe. However, not all high homicide areas are associated with a high prevalence of firearm homicide. For example, some sub-regions with relatively high homicide rates, such as Eastern Europe and Southern Africa, have a relatively low share of homicides by firearm, while others, such as Southern Europe and Northern Africa, have lower homicide rates but higher shares of homicides committed by firearm. In addition to weapons, the consumption of alcohol and/or illicit drugs increases one's risk of becoming a victim or perpetrator of violence. In Sweden and Finland, for example, over half of all homicide offenders were intoxicated with alcohol when they committed homicide. In Australia, recent data suggests that nearly half of all homicide incidents were preceded by alcohol consumption 2 Lethality of a weapon depends on the type and calibre of firearm. Whether or not a victim survives a gunshot wound is often dependent on other factors, such as the availability and efficiency of health care systems. For more, see Alvazzi del Frate, A. (2012). Small Arms Survey, Moving

Targets: chapter 3. 16 GLOBAL STUDY on Homicide Homicide mechanism, by region (2012 or latest year) Source: UNODC Homicide Statistics (2013) and IHME (2010). by the victim or the perpetrator, or both. Illicit drugs can affect homicide levels in different ways, but the psychopharmacological effects of certain illicit drugs, such as cocaine and amphetaminetype stimulants, are more linked to violence than others and can have an impact on homicide similar to that caused by alcohol, as indicated by data from some countries. As well as violence associated with the consumption of illicit drugs, violence associated with the functioning of illicit drug markets can also drive homicide levels, often due to competition between involved parties. Studies and available data indicate that the cultivation, production, trafficking and sale of illicit drugs may be accompanied by high levels of violence and homicide. However, this relationship does not hold in all situations because the modus operandi of organized criminal groups, as well as the response by State authorities, can determine actual levels of homicidal violence involved in drug trafficking. Homicide, violence and conflict In countries emerging from conflict, it is often difficult to disentangle lethal violence that is an aftereffect of conflict, or a lower-intensity continuation of conflict, from violence of a different nature, particularly if the conflict has not been fully resolved. Reducing violence in countries emerging from conflict goes beyond the need to address the roots of the conflict, to include the prevention of surges in violence resulting from organized crime and interpersonal violence, which can flourish in settings with weak rule of law. This study presents findings from selected countries based on the availability of data, which show that crime is an important component of violence in countries emerging from conflict, and that violence related to crime can become a significant factor in the overall security situation in such countries. The analysis is based on the situations in Afghanistan, Haiti, Iraq, Liberia, Sierra Leone and South Sudan, which have all had different

experiAfrica (54 countries)
Americas (36 countries)

SOCIO-POLITICAL HOMICIDE In contrast to the two other homicide typologies, this type of homicide can be seen to be the outcome of the socio-political agenda of its perpetrator(s). As its name implies, socio-political homicide may be politically motivated, or particular individuals or groups may be targeted due to their race, ethnicity, gender, religion, sexuality or status, amongst others. For example, homicides linked to hate crimes or acts of terror are both considered to be part of this typology. In all such cases, a social dimension (such as the management of diversity in society) or a power-related struggle comes into play. Data availability on socio-political homicide is very limited, either because some killings of this nature are often excluded from homicide counts at the country level or, when included, they cannot be statistically identified due to a lack of information about the motive and context of such killings. For these reasons, this section provides a snapshot of some of their

manifestations. Hate Crimes Crimes motivated by the perpetrator's bias against the victim's race, religion, ethnic origin, sexual orientation or disability, amongst others, hate crimes can also be thought of as products of social prejudice. Ingrained attitudes may promote an atmosphere that condones violence against marginalized segments of society, often resulting in "message crimes" that instil fear or terror based on prejudicial attitudes.30 As they not only affect indi- 28 Some mass homicides are not represented in the data because they have been reported by law enforcement agencies in separate records, with a maximum of 11 victims per record. For example, an incident with 32 victims was reported as 4 separate incidents, with 10 victims each in the

"first" three incidents and two in the "fourth" incident. The net result is that these data somewhat over-count the number of mass murder incidents and somewhat undercount the average number of victims per mass murder incident. 29 Bureau of Justice Statistics, United States (2013). 30 Mouzos, J. and S. Thompson (2000), in Australian

Institute 95.4% 3.8% 0.6% 0.2% 1 vicϴm 2 vicϴms 3 vicϴms 4 or more vicϴms Fig. 2.2.14: Number of homicide cases with four or more victims; and related number of victims, United States (2002-2011) Source: Bureau of Justice Statistics, United States (2013). Fig. 2.2.15: Average percentage distribution of homicide cases, by number of victims, United States (2002-2011) Source: Bureau of Justice Statistics, United States (2013). 0 50 100 150 200 250 2002 2003 2004 2005 2006 2007 2008 2009 2010 2011 Number of homicide cases with four or more victims Number of victims in homicide cases with four or more victims 59 THE MANY FACES OF HOMICIDE vidual victims, but also members of the victim's group and even society as a whole, such crimes are threats to social cohesion.31 Hate crimes can consist of a variety of violent and non-violent crimes, ranging from threats and robbery to rape, with homicide their most extreme manifestation. Accurately identifying, classifying and recording a homicide as a hate crime can be particularly challenging, as it requires the determination of a causal link

between an offender's prejudice towards the victim and their act of lethal violence. There are relatively few cases of known hate crimerelated homicide, and studies of this issue are few in number. For example, gender-based killing due to sexual orientation and gender identity is a phenomenon that has only recently been documented and only very limited, often anecdotal, data are available.32 That said, the United Nations Special Rapporteur on Extrajudicial, Summary or Arbitrary Executions has documented murders believed to have been committed on the grounds of sexual orientation or gender identity.33 Furthermore, according to the United Nations Special Rapporteur on Violence Against Women, homicides of transgender people were documented in 816 cases in 55 countries between January 2008 and December 2011.34 Many of those homicides are believed to be the result of hate-based violence, but data on motivation are extremely limited, thus it is not possible to identify all of them as being specifically due to the victim's identification as transgender. In South Africa, information from case studies has indicated that 31 lesbians have been murdered in homophobic attacks since 1998.35 An academic study in Australia that examined gay-hate related homicides in New South Wales identified approximately four gay men killed due to their sexual orientation each year over the 10-year period covered by the study (1989-1999).36 of Criminology: Trends and Issues in crime and criminal justice. No. 155. 31 Bleich, E. (2007), in American Behavioural Scientist, 51. Also, for example, in some case law, family members of victims were also considered victims, and sometimes granted compensation. See Inter-American Court of Human Rights, (2009). 32 United Nations General Assembly (2012). A/HRC/20/16. 33 United Nations General Assembly, Human Rights Council (2013) A/HRC/24/23. 34 United Nations General Assembly (2012). Op.Cit. 35 Wesley, T. (2012), in BUWA! A Journal on African

Women's Experiences. 36 Mouzos, J. and S. Thompson. (2000). Op.Cit. Other social prejudices, such as those based on race, religion or

ethnic origin, can also result in lethal violence. When looking at the scarce data available, it can be noted that in three European countries which do have data, foreign residents are over-represented among homicide victims (see figure 2.3.1). Such data cannot be strictly interpreted as hate crime-related, as it is not known whether those victims were specifically targeted due to their membership of a racial, ethnic or religious group, but it does indicate that foreign residents can face a higher risk of victimization than the general population. As mentioned earlier, homicide is the most extreme manifestation of hate-related violence. Other than lethal violence, crimes motivated by bias or prejudice are also difficult to identify, as many victims of hate crimes are reluctant to report them, which means that many hate crimes remain invisible.37 Acts of terror Often resulting in multiple victims, acts of terror leading to death are a global phenomenon but also a challenging category to examine statistically, as very few countries produce data on such deaths. Those with multiple victims, which result in mass murder incidents, may be classified in different ways based on varying definitions. 37 For an overview of hate crimes in Europe, see European Union Agency for Fundamental Rights (2012). Fig. 2.3.1: Homicide rate among total population and among foreign residents, selected European countries (2010) Source: UN-CTS (2011); data on Austria include attempted homicides. 0.0 0.5 1.0 1.5 2.0 2.5 3.0 3.5 4.0 Austria Finland Italy ZĂłĞĐĞᵭ ĐŽĐzůĂⵙŽŶ Total populaⵙon Foreign residents

60 GLOBAL STUDY on Homicide From a conceptual perspective, the label "intentional homicide" is certainly broad enough to encompass such deaths, and whilst perpetrators may face additional charges, such as acts of terrorism, acts against the State, or even crimes against humanity, the core act still concerns the unlawful intentional killing of another. That said, in national recording practices, such deaths are not always recorded and counted as intentional homicide, or in other cases, though considered as such, a specific statistical count is not available.38 Unlawful killings by law enforcement authorities Some of

the most challenging incidents to identify and account for statistically as "intentional homicide" are unlawful killings by law enforcement authorities, including the police. The State has an obligation to safeguard life:39 the use of lethal force by the police is strictly limited by international human rights law and relevant standards, and is to be applied only in situations where it is necessary to protect life.40 Deaths occurring as a result of the necessary and proportionate use of force by law enforcement officers do not constitute unlawful killings. Unplanned killings that result from excessive use of force in law enforcement operations may be unlawful, although they would not qualify 38 Country practice varies as to whether such deaths are included in police homicide statistics. For example, neither the 3,000+ victims of the attacks on the United States on 11 September 2001, nor the nearly 200 killed in terrorist attacks on 11 March 2004 in Madrid were recorded as homicides in national criminal justice statistics. By contrast, the 52 victims of the 7 July 2005 London bombings and the 77 victims of the terror events of 22 July 2011 in Norway were included in official police statistics as homicides. Homicide statistics in India include murder related to "terrorist/extremist" violence. 39

This obligation of the State consists of three main aspects: a) the duty to refrain, by its agents, from unlawful killing; b) the duty to investigate suspicious deaths; and c) in certain circumstances, a positive obligation to take steps to prevent the avoidable loss of life. (For example, see European Court of Human Rights (2013); Ovey, C. and R. White (2002). 40 Principle 9 of the Basic Principles on the Use of Force and Firearms by Law Enforcement Officials (1990) provides for instance: "Law enforcement officials shall not use firearms against persons except in self-defence or defence of others against the imminent threat of death or serious injury, to prevent the perpetration of a particularly serious crime involving grave threat to life, to arrest a person presenting such a danger and resisting their authority, or to prevent his or her escape, and only when less extreme means are insufficient to achieve these

objectives. In any event, intentional lethal use of firearms may only be made when strictly unavoidable in order to protect life." Article 3 of the Code of Conduct for Law Enforcement Officials, adopted by the General Assembly in its resolution 34/169, states that "Law enforcement officials may use force only when strictly necessary and to the extent required for the performance of their duty." Principle 3 of the Interpol Code of Conduct for Law Enforcement Officials states that "Officers must never knowingly use more force than is reasonable, nor should they abuse their authority." as intentional homicides in the absence of any element of intentionality. Among the special procedures of the Human Rights Council, the United Nations Special Rapporteur on Extrajudicial, Summary or Arbitrary Executions holds the mandate for examining situations of unlawful killing by the police, among other situations of extrajudicial, summary or arbitrary executions.41 For example, killings by the police may occur in situations where the police are not pursuing law enforcement objectives, such as attempts at extortion that may escalate into extrajudicial killings; engaging in "social cleansing" operations and intentionally killing criminals or members of marginalized groups; or in even more extreme situations, where police are operating as a militia or death squad.42 All such cases should be counted as intentional homicides, consistently with the standard definition, but little statistical information is available on such homicides, often due to a lack of recording and tracking, as well as a lack of investigation into the nature of the killings, all of which hamper data collection efforts. Findings, conclusions and recommendations of the United Nations Special Rapporteur are submitted to the Human Rights Council and the General Assembly, and constitute both a source of data and examples.43 Mob violence/Vigilantism Cases of

"vigilante" or "mob" violence have been reported in different places around the world. The nature of these acts can vary widely, but at their core they are "killings carried out in violation of the law by private individuals with the purported aim of crime control, or the control of perceived deviant or immoral behaviour."44 Although vigilantism has occurred across the world, recent studies have focused on this phenomenon in Africa, the Americas and Asia.45 For example, in Uganda in 2010, there were 438 fatalities due to acts of mob justice, accounting for 25 41 United Nations General Assembly, Human Rights Council (2011). A/HRC/RES/17/5 42 United Nations General Assembly, Human Rights Council (2010). A/HRC/14/24/Add.8. Para. 9. 43 See, for example, United Nations General Assembly, Human Rights Council. Reports of the Special Rapporteur on extrajudicial, summary or arbitrary executions. For example: A/HRC/21/49; A/HRC/22/67; A/HRC/23/51. 44 United Nations General Assembly, Human Rights Council (2009). A/64/187. Para. 15. 45 See United Nations General Assembly, Human Rights Council (2009). 61 THE MANY FACES OF HOMICIDE per cent of all homicides in the country.46 The most common victims of mob violence are suspected criminals, generally young males, especially those suspected of committing theft.47 Other targets of "vigilante justice" include suspected murderers, members of gangs or organized criminal groups, suspected or convicted sexual offenders, suspected "witches" and street children.48 Mob violence can indicate a population's lack of faith or trust in the rule of law and its implementing institutions to provide justice. If people feel the criminal justice system is not legitimate, is corrupt or unresponsive, they may feel obliged to take matters into their own hands to enforce laws. For example, in a study of formal and informal dispute resolution systems in poorer, rural areas of South America, vigilantism appeared to be five times greater in communities where informal mechanisms of justice were not functioning.49 Shooting the messengers: the killing of journalists and humanitarian aid workers As professionals who often work in insecure environments, mostly in response to natural or manmade disasters, journalists and aid workers are both prone to certain risks that can threaten their safety and even their lives.

Journalists, as purveyors of information who seek out and report the news from around the world, often venture into the darkest corners to shed light on current events. A considerable number of them are subjected to intimidation, physical violence, kidnapping or illegal detention in direct relation to their work and, in extreme cases, they can be killed because of their professional activity. Some are killed in war or conflict zones or in situations of civil unrest, while others are the specific targets of homicidal violence. It is challenging to disentangle the various motives behind such killings, but some data are available. According to UNESCO, since 1992 there have been 984 documented cases of killings of journalists, with over 600 of them occurring in the last 10 years.50 UNESCO has also drawn attention to the 46 Ugandan Police Force (2011). P. 7. 47 United Nations General Assembly, Human Rights Council (2009). Para. 58. 48 Ibid. Para. 64. 49 UNDP (2006). P. 14. 50 United Nations General Assembly, Human Rights Council fact that there is often impunity for many of the abuses against journalists,51 which, in conjunction with a climate of violence, generates censorship, depriving citizens of the information they need to make informed decisions. Besides UNESCO, the Committee to Protect Journalists (CPJ)52 also tracks events around the world in which journalists are killed because of their professional activities. The statistics kept by each organization differ due to varying definitions as to who exactly is considered a journalist and what is considered a "killing in the line of duty"53 (2013). Para. 5; and UNESCO (2013). UNESCO condemns the killing of journalists. 51 See United Nations (2012). Second Inter-Agency Meeting on the Safety of Journalists and the Issue of Impunity. 52 The Committee to Protect Journalists (CPJ) is an independent, non-profit organization that promotes press freedom worldwide. 53 CPJ keeps statistics on the death of every journalist whom it is reasonably certain was killed in direct reprisal for his or her work; was killed in crossfire during combat situations; or was killed while carrying out a dangerous assignment such as coverage of a street protest.

Journalists killed in accidents such as car or plane crashes are not included. UNESCO uses a broad definition and it refers to the killing of reporters, camera operators, photojournalists, television presenters, columnists, editors, broadcasters, radio presenters and other members of the media. Given these definitions, it is not always possible to differentiate between journalists who were victims of intentional homicide and those who were victims of war/conflict, based on these sources.

Measures to control knife-carrying in the United Kingdom

Noting the severity of knife-related homicide, particularly among young people, the United Kingdom enacted the Violent Crime Reduction Act in 2006. Among its many provisions, it included raising the minimum age for buying a knife from 16 to 18 years of age, and increasing the maximum sentence for carrying a knife without good reason from two to four yearsa In addition, the United Kingdom launched the "Tackling Knives Action Programme (TKAP)" in 2008, in response to a number of knife homicides involving teenage victims.

Police in areas of greatest concern introduced a range of enforcement, education and prevention initiatives aimed at reducing youth knife violence. The programme ran from June 2008 to March 2010 and demonstrated positive reductions in the number of homicide victims and suspects in the areas in which it was implemented, though the reductions were not proportionately higher in programme areas than elsewhere, as reductions of serious youth violence were noted across the country from 2007 to 2010.b a Government of the United Kingdom (2006). Violent Crime Reduction Act. b For more on the TKAP, see Ward, L, Nicholas S. and M. Willoughby (2011). S Fig. 3.8: Average percentage of homicides, by homicide mechanism, Scotland (2003-2013) Source: Scottish Government (2013). Firearm Sharp object Blunt instrument

Hiṭng/Kicking Other/Unknown 9% 38% 9% 20% 24% 72 GLOBAL STUDY on Homicide Alcohol A serious threat to public health in many countries, alcohol can affect different types of interpersonal violence, including various types of interpersonal homicide. The link between alcohol and violence involves a causal chain that binds together alcohol consumption and other

aforementioned factors to form a relationship that may be more conditional than deterministic.21 While violence levels, including homicide rates, are influenced by the volume of alcohol consumption, they are even more influenced by patterns of alcohol consumption, with a number of studies indicating, for example, that hazardous drinking patterns are strongly associated with homicide rates.22 Findings made by the European Homicide Monitor suggest that 82 per cent of homicide offenders in Finland in 2003-2006 were intoxicated with alcohol when they committed murder, whereas that was the case for slightly more than half of homicide offenders in Sweden.23 This research also suggests that the difference between total homicide rates in Finland and Sweden can to a large extent be attributed to alcohol-related homicides (see figure 3.9).24 Australia also has available data on the consumption of alcohol by homicide victims and offenders. In 2008-2010, nearly half of all homicide incidents were preceded by alcohol consumption by the victim or the perpetrator, or both.25 Elsewhere, in cases reviewed in the southern Indian State of Odisha from 2006-2011, 30.2 per cent of homicide victims were found to have a positive blood alcohol content.26 The consumption of alcohol, particularly at "harmful" levels, is a major risk factor for homicides between partners. As an example, a Finnish study on intimate partner homicides between 21 For a review of the many elements involved in the relationship between alcohol and violence, see Bye, E.K. (2012), in Handbook of European Homicide Research: Patterns, explanations and country studies. 22 See Rossow, I. (2000), National Institute for Alcohol and Drug Research, Norway; Bye, E. K. (2008), in Homicide Studies 12(1); Rehm, J., et al. (2004), World Health Organization. 23 Homicide in Finland, the Netherlands and Sweden: A first study on the European Homicide Monitor data (2011). 24 Lehti, M. and J. Kivivuori, (2005), in Nordisk alcohol- and narko-tikatidskrift, 22. Pp. 5-18. 25 Australian Institute of Criminology (2013). 26 Mohanty, S. et al. (2013), in Forensic Medicine and Anatomy Research 1(2). 2002 and 2010 showed that 73 per cent of all male offenders and 77 per cent of all female offenders were under the influence of alcohol at the time of the homicide. The study also noted that 62 per cent of the victims of

male offenders and 77 per cent of the victims of female offenders were also intoxicated with alcohol.27 Links between these phenomena are manifold and research has suggested that the use of alcohol increases both the occurrence and severity of intimate partner violence for the following reasons: alcohol use has a direct effect on both cognitive and physical function, reducing inhibition and leaving people less capable of negotiating a nonviolent resolution to conflicts within relationships; excessive drinking by one partner can exacerbate financial difficulties, childcare problems, infidelity or other family stressors, resulting in increased tensions in a relationships and the potential risk of violence between partners; and individual and societal beliefs that alcohol causes aggression can excuse or condone violent behaviour after drinking, and the use of alcohol can be an excuse for violent behaviour. 27 Kivivuori, J. and M. Lehti (2012), in Homicide Studies 16 (1): P.60. Fig. 3.9: Annual victimization rates of alcohol-related and non-alcoholrelated homicides, Finland and Sweden (2003-2006) Source: European Homicide Monitor. 0 0.5 1 1.5 2 2.5 Finland Sweden ZĂłĞĐĞä   ĐŽĐZůĂΘŽŶ

Unknown Not alcohol related (all persons involved were sober) To some extent alcohol-related (some persons involved were intoxicated) Strongly alcohol-related (all persons involved were intoxicated) 73 HOMICIDE MECHANISMS AND ENA

Domestic Violence:

Importance of Understanding Domestic Violence

The U.S. Surgeon General recently declared domestic violence to be the number one health concern in our country today. Understanding the definition of domestic violence can help you take action against it. Some people may not even realize that they are inflicting domestic violence on someone else. On the flipside, victims will not know to take action against their abusers if they do not realize that what is being inflicted upon them is, in fact, domestic violence. Likewise, friends and loved ones of victims are in a better place to help if they understand what domestic

violence looks like. Therefore, it is important that people understand the definition of domestic violence and the many forms it can take.

Definition of Domestic Violence

According to the United States Department of Justices **Office on Violence Against Women**, the definition of domestic violence is a pattern of abusive behavior in any relationship that is used by one partner to gain or maintain control over another intimate partner. Many forms of abuse are included in the definition of domestic violence:

- **Physical abuse** can include hitting, biting, slapping, battering, shoving, punching, pulling hair, burning, cutting, pinching, etc. (any type of violent behavior inflicted on the victim). Physical abuse also includes denying someone medical treatment and forcing drug/alcohol use on someone.
- **Sexual abuse** occurs when the abuser coerces or attempts to coerce the victim into having sexual contact or sexual behavior without the victims consent. This often takes the form of marital rape, attacking sexual body parts, physical violence that is followed by forcing sex, sexually demeaning the victim, or even

telling sexual jokes at the victims expense.

- **Emotional abuse** involves invalidating or deflating the victims sense of self-worth and/or self-esteem. Emotional abuse often takes the form of constant criticism, name-calling, injuring the victims relationship with his/her children, or interfering with the victims abilities.

- **Economic abuse** takes place when the abuser makes or tries to make the victim financially reliant. Economic abusers often seek to maintain total control over financial resources, withhold the victims access to funds, or prohibit the victim from going to school or work.

- **Psychological abuse** involves the abuser invoking fear through intimidation; threatening to physically hurt himself/herself, the victim, children, the victims family or friends, or the pets; destruction of property; injuring the pets; isolating the victim from loved ones; and prohibiting the victim from going to school or work.

- **Threats** to hit, injure, or use a weapon are a form of psychological abuse.

- **Stalking** can include following the victim, spying, watching, harassing, showing up at the victims home or work, sending gifts, collecting information, making phone calls, leaving written messages, or appearing at a person's home or workplace. These acts individually are typically legal, but any of these behaviors done continuously results in stalkinga crime.

- **Cyberstalking** refers to online action or repeated emailing that inflicts substantial emotional distress in the recipient.

Who Can be Victims of Domestic Violence

The definition of domestic violence goes on to say that victims can include anyone, regardless of socioeconomic background, education level, race, age, sexual orientation, religion, or gender. Domestic violence used to be referred to as wife abuse. However, this term was abandoned when the definition of domestic violence changed to recognize that wives are not the only ones who can fall victim to domestic violence. The definition of domestic violence now recognizes that victims can be:

- Spouses
- Sexual/Dating/Intimate partners
- Family members
- Children
- Cohabitants

Many people think that a victim of domestic violence can only obtain a protective order against his or her spouse. This is actually a myth. Most states allow victims of abusive cohabitant lovers to obtain protective orders (also referred to as temporary restraining orders or emergency protective orders). Some states allow victims of abusive adult relatives, roommates, or even non-cohabitating partners to obtain protective orders. The laws in each state are different. As recognition for the need for protection grows in each state, the law evolves to reflect it, so be sure to check the most updated laws in your state.

Dating Violence

Dating violence is another form of domestic violence. The Violence Against Women Act defines dating violence according to the relationship between the abuser and victim. Dating violence is committed by a person in a social, romantic, or intimate relationship with the victim. The existence of such relationship is determined using the following factors:

- The length of the relationship
- The type of relationship
- The partners frequency of interaction

Help for Victims

- National Domestic Violence Hotline
1-800-799-SAFE (7233)
1-800-787-3224
(TTY) www.ndvh.org
- Rape, Abuse, and Incest National Network
1-800-656-HOPE
(4673) www.rainn.org
- National Sexual Violence Resource Center
(NSVRC) 1-877-739-3895
www.nsvrc.org
- National Center for Victims of Crime, Stalking Resource Center 1-800-394-2255 1-800-211-7996 (TTY) www.ncvc.org

- National Teen Dating Abuse Helpline
1-866-331-9474
1-866-331-8453 TTY
www.loveisrespect.org

Help for Abusers

- EMERGE: A Men's Counseling Service
617-547-9879
www.emergedv.com
- See more at:
http://family.findlaw.com/domestic-violence/what-is-domestic-violence.html#sthash.rVDoO0eL.dpuf

Source: Findlaw

Retired Law Enforcement Captain:

Mr. H (Take Notice) Must be included and credited for Job well done as an acting Chief in critical department time most needed.

It happened to be on the page as an extra added footnote.

Fullerton police Department:

History

Chiefs of the Fullerton Police Department

Date	Chief of Department
1904 July	Marshal Charles E. Ruddock
1910 April	Marshal Roderick D. Stone
1912	Marshal William

November	French
1918 August	Chief Vernon Myers
1921 August	Chief Arthur L. Eeles
1925 April	Chief O. W. Wilson
1925 December	Chief Thomas K. Winter
1927 December	Chief James M. Pearson
1940 April	Chief John C. Gregory
1951 February	Chief Ernest E. Garner
1957 November	Chief Wayne H. Bornhoft
1977 September	Chief Martin Hairabedian
1987 March	Chief Philip

	Goehring
1993 March	Chief Patrick McKinley
2009 April	Chief Michael Sellers*
2012 January	Acting Chief Dan Hughes
2013 January	Chief Dan Hughes

- Sellers began paid medical leave August 2011 and retired in February 2012. Kevin Hamilton was named acting chief in his place.

Source: ONLINE Wikipedia the free Encyclopedia

FBI Uniform Crime Report

The Uniform Crime Reporting (UCR) Program has been the starting place for law enforcement executives, students of criminal justice, researchers, members of the media, and the public at large seeking information on crime in the nation. The program was conceived in 1929 by the International Association of Chiefs of Police to meet the need for reliable uniform crime statistics for the nation. In 1930, the FBI was tasked with collecting, publishing, and archiving those statistics.

Today, four annual publications, *Crime in the United States*, *National Incident-Based Reporting System*, *Law Enforcement Officers Killed and Assaulted*,

and *Hate Crime Statistics* are produced from data received from over 18,000 city, university/college, county, state, tribal, and federal law enforcement agencies voluntarily participating in the program. The crime data are submitted either through a state UCR Program or directly to the FBI's UCR Program.

In addition to these reports, information is available on the Law Enforcement Officers Killed and Assaulted (LEOKA) Program and the Hate Crime Statistics Program, as well as the traditional Summary Reporting System (SRS) and the National Incident-Based Reporting System (NIBRS). Also available—FAQs about the UCR Program.

The FBI is undertaking a wholesale redesign and redevelopment of the system that has supported the FBI's UCR Program for more than 30 years. In support of this initiative, the FBI created the UCR Redevelopment Project (UCRRP). **Details**

FBI Report on Police Officers Killed in 2013

Number of police officers killed on duty in 2014 jumps nearly 90%.

Fifty-one law enforcement officers were feloniously killed in the line of duty in 2014, according to preliminary FBI data. An additional 44 police officers were killed accidentally, with most of the deaths occurring in the Southern region of the US.

Most of the criminal fatalities were from firearms, while the accidental deaths were largely the result of car accidents, the FBI said.

The statistics released Monday show an 89 percent increase over the 27 officers killed in 2013. Broken down into regions – 17 were killed in the South, 14 in the West, eight in the Midwest, eight in the Northeast, and four in

Puerto Rico. The 51 officers died from injuries sustained in 48 separate incidents.

In a video message, FBI Director James

Comey referenced the *"especially challenging relationship between law enforcement and the communities we serve"* when announcing the statistics, adding they represent a *"shocking increase."*
He called on law enforcement to

"do our absolute best to try and see clearly those people we serve and to look for opportunities to have them see us."

Of the criminal deaths, 46 of the 51 were the result of the use of firearms. Handguns accounted for 32 deaths, with 11 incidents involving the use of rifles and three with shotguns. Four police officers were killed by vehicles and one officer was killed by an offender's use of hands, fists, or feet.

The incidents that led up to the officers deaths involved answering disturbance calls, conducting traffic stops or pursuits, ambushes, investigating a suspicious person, during investigations, and handling persons with mental illness.

Five of the 51 officers killed had fired their own weapons and six attempted to use their guns. One was killed with his own weapon, seven had theirs stolen and 35 died while wearing body armor

There were fewer accidental deaths in 2014 than in 2013, however. Of the 44 officers who died in 2014, compared to 49 in 2013, 28 died in automobile accidents (15 were wearing their seatbelts), six in motorcycle accidents, and five were struck by vehicles. Accidental shootings took two lives, and three others died in separate incidents of drowning, blunt force trauma and smoke inhalation.

The FBI said statistics from 1980-2014 show an average of 64 law enforcement officers are killed criminally per year. Last year's 27 deaths marked the lowest record during a 35-year period.

Final statistics will be published on the FBI's website in the fall via the Department of Justice.

FBI Releases 2013 Statistics on Law Enforcement Officers Killed and Assaulted

FBI San DiegoDecember 02, 2014	• Darrell Foxworth(858) 8302

On January 15, 2013, an officer with the Galt, California Police Department was killed while investigating a suspicious person/circumstance. On February 7, 2013, a Riverside Police Department (RPD) Officer was shot and killed and another wounded during an ambush. On February 12, 2013, the same suspect involved in the February 7, 2013 incident shot and killed a San Bernardino County Sheriff's Department Deputy (SBCSD) during a tactical situation. On February 26, 2013, two Santa Cruz Police Department detectives were killed while attempting an arrest. These are some of the killings included in the FBI's recently released *Law Enforcement Officers Killed and Assaulted* (LEOKA) 2013 report.

According to the LEOKA report, these officers were among the 76 men and women killed in the line of duty during 2013—27 died as a result of felonious acts, and 49 died in accidents. Another 49,851 law enforcement officers were victims of line-of-duty assaults.

According to statistics collected by the FBI, 76 law enforcement officers were killed in line-of-duty incidents in 2013. Of these, 27 law enforcement officers died as a result of felonious acts, and 49 officers died in accidents. In addition, 49,851 officers were victims of line-of-duty assaults. Comprehensive data tables about these incidents and brief narratives describing the fatal attacks and selected assaults resulting in injury are included in the 2013 edition of *Law Enforcement Officers Killed and Assaulted*.

Among the report's findings for 2013:

Of the 27 officers feloniously killed, 16 were on assigned vehicle patrol duty when the incidents occurred, and all but one of the 27 officers was killed with a firearm.

Circumstances surrounding the deaths of these 27 officers included arrest situations, ambushes, investigations of suspicious persons, disturbance calls, tactical situations, traffic pursuits or stops, and investigative activities.

Law enforcement agencies identified 28 alleged assailants in connection with the felonious line-of-duty deaths (20 had prior criminal records).

Of the 49 officers accidentally killed, 23 died as a result of automobile accidents.

Of the nearly 49,851 officers assaulted during 2013, the largest percentage of victim officers (31.2 percent) were responding to disturbance calls (family quarrels, bar fights, etc.) when the incidents occurred.

Overview

- In 2013, 49 law enforcement officers died as the result of accidents that occurred in the line of duty.

- Accidental line-of-duty deaths of law enforcement officers occurred in 22 states.

- Of the officers accidentally killed, 24 were employed by city police departments, 15 were employed by county agencies, 8 were employed by state agencies, and 2 were employed by federal agencies.

- By region, 31 officers who were accidentally killed were employed by agencies in the South, 9 by agencies in the West, 5 by agencies in the Northeast, and 4 by agencies in the Midwest.

Victim profile

- The average age of the officers who died accidentally in 2013 was 41 years.

- The average length of law enforcement service for the officers accidentally killed in the line of duty was 13 years.

- Of the officers who were accidentally killed, 41 were white, 6 were black, and race was not reported for 2 officers.

- All 49 of the officers were male.

Circumstances

Of the officers who were accidentally killed in the line of duty in 2013:

- 23 died as a result of automobile accidents.

- 9 were struck by vehicles.

- 4 officers died in motorcycle accidents.

- 4 were killed in falls.

- 2 were accidentally shot as a result of crossfire, mistaken for subject, or other firearm mishaps.

- 2 officers drowned.

- 1 died in an aircraft accident.

- 4 officers died in other types of accidents.

Of the 9 officers struck by vehicles:

- 8 were directing traffic, assisting motorists, etc.

- 1 was executing a traffic stop, roadblock, etc.

Assignments

- 24 of the on-duty officers accidentally killed in 2013 were alone at the time of the accidents.

- 21 on-duty officers had assistance at the time of their fatal accidents.

- 4 officers were off duty, but acting in an official capacity, at the times of their fatal accidents.

Months, days, and times of incidents:

- In 2013, the greatest number of accidents resulting in the deaths of law enforcement officers (9) occurred in May.

- More officers were fatally injured in accidents on Fridays in 2013, with 12 officers accidentally killed.

- 16 officers were killed as a result of accidents occurring between 12:01 a.m. and noon.

- 30 officers were fatally injured in accidents that occurred between 12:01 p.m. and midnight.

Felonious Deaths

The 27 felonious deaths occurred in 16 states. The number of officers killed as a result of criminal acts in 2013 decreased by 22 when compared with the 49 officers who were feloniously killed in 2012. The five- and 10-year comparisons show a decrease of 21 felonious deaths compared with the 2009 figure (48 officers) and a decrease of 30 deaths

compared with 2004 data
(57 officers).

Officer Profiles: The average age of the officers who were feloniously killed was 39 years. The victim officers had served in law enforcement for an average of 13 years at the time of the fatal incidents. Twenty-five of the officers were male, and two were female. Twenty-five of the officers were white, and two were black.

Circumstances: Of the 27 officers feloniously killed, six were killed in arrest situations, five were investigating suspicious persons or circumstances, five were ambushed, four were involved in tactical situations, four were answering disturbance calls, and two were conducting traffic pursuits/stops. One was conducting an investigative activity, such as surveillance, a search, or an interview.

Weapons: Offenders used firearms to kill 26 of the 27 victim officers. Of these 26 officers, 18 were slain with handguns, five with rifles, and three with shotguns. One officer was killed with a vehicle used as a weapon.

Regions: Fifteen of the felonious deaths occurred in the South, six in the West, four in the Midwest, and two in the Northeast.

Suspects: Law enforcement agencies identified 28 alleged assailants in connection with the felonious line-of-duty deaths. Twenty of the assailants had prior criminal arrests, and six of the offenders were under judicial supervision at the time of the felonious incidents.

Accidental Deaths

Forty-nine law enforcement officers were killed accidentally while performing their duties in 2013. The majority (23 officers) were killed in automobile accidents. The number of accidental line-of-duty deaths increased by one from the 2012 total (48 officers).

Officer Profiles: The average age of the officers who were accidentally killed was 41 years; the average number of years the victim officers had served in law enforcement was 13. All 49 of the officers were male. Forty-one of the officers were white, six were black, and race was not reported for two officers.

Circumstances: Of the 49 officers accidentally killed, 23 died as a result of automobile accidents, nine were struck by vehicles, four officers died in motorcycle accidents, four officers were killed in falls, two were accidentally shot, two drowned, one died in an aircraft accident, and four officers died in other types of duty-related accidents. Seatbelt usage was reported for 22 of the 23 officers killed in automobile accidents. Of these, 14 officers were not wearing seatbelts, three of whom were seated in parked patrol vehicles. Eight officers were wearing their seatbelts at the times of the accidents.

Regions: Thirty-one of the accidental deaths occurred in the South, nine in the West, five in the Northeast, and 4 in the Midwest.

Assaults

In 2013, of the 49,851 officers assaulted while performing their duties, 29.2 percent were injured. The largest percentage of victim officers (31.2 percent) were assaulted while responding to disturbance calls. Assailants used personal weapons (hands, fists, feet, etc.) in 79.8 percent of the incidents, firearms in 4.5 percent of incidents, and knives or other cutting instruments in 1.8 percent of the incidents. Other types of dangerous weapons were used in 13.9 percent of assaults. Expanded assault details have been included in the 2013 publication. Data for assaults during which officers were injured with firearms or knives/other cutting instruments are located in new tables, figures, and selected narratives.

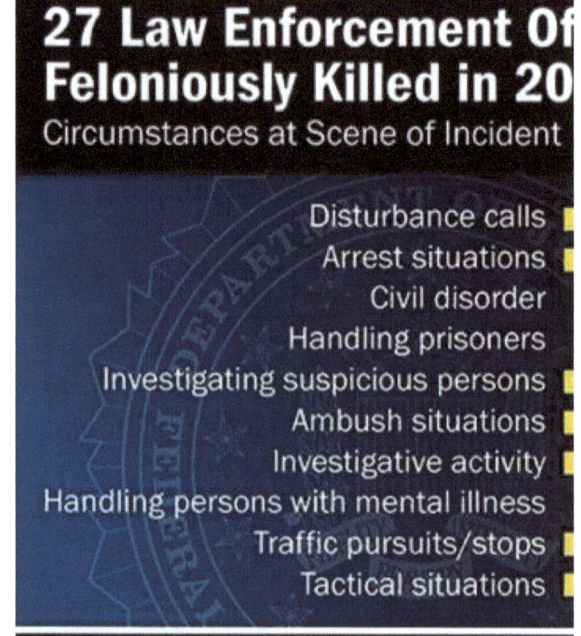

The LEOKA publication, released by the FBI's Uniform Crime Reporting (UCR) Program, contains data on duly-sworn city, university/college, county, state, tribal, and federal law enforcement officers who, at the time of the incidents, met the following criteria:

- They were working in an official capacity, whether on or off duty;
- They had full arrest powers;
- They ordinarily wore/carried a badge and a firearm; and
- They were paid from government funds set aside specifically for sworn law enforcement representatives.

The information in the report comes from various sources—the law enforcement agencies participating in the UCR Program, FBI field offices, and several non-profit organizations, such as the Concerns of Police Survivors and the National Law Enforcement Officers Memorial Fund.

The goal of the FBI's LEOKA program is to provide data and training that help keep law enforcement officers safe as they serve and protect our nation's communities. To view the entire report please visit www.fbi.gov.

www.ingramcontent.com/pod-product-compliance
Lightning Source LLC
Chambersburg PA
CBHW040744200526
45159CB00023B/1691